Poetry for Young People

William Shakespeare

Edited by David Scott Kastan & Marina Kastan
Illustrated by Glenn Harrington

Sterling Publishing Company, Inc.
New York

For John Regis and, of course, for SEVWK

—David and Marina

To Evan and Sean—for whom Queen Mab's coach waits till your little noses grow, and Christine, who
knows my mind true, and of course, Mom and Dad.

—Glenn

Library of Congress Cataloging-in-Publication Data Available

Shakespeare, William , 1564-1616.
[Poems. Selection]
William Shakespeare / edited by David Scott Kastan & Marina Kastan;
illustrated by Glen Harrington.
p. cm. – (Poetry for young people)
Includes index.
Summary: Introduces the poetry of William Shakespeare through a sampling of sonnets and
excerpts from his plays.
ISBN 0-8069-4344-0
1. Children's poetry, English. [1. English poetry.] I. Kastan, David Scott. II. Kastan, Marina.
III. Harrington, Glen, ill. IV. Title. V. Series.
PR2771.K37 2000
821'.3—dc21   00–028489

3 5 7 9 10 8 6 4 2

Published by Sterling Publishing Company, Inc.
387 Park Avenue South, New York, N.Y. 10016
Editorial matter © 2000 by David Scott Kastan and Marina Kastan
Illustrations © 2000 by Glenn Harrington
Portrait by Gerard Soest on page 4 courtesy of The Shakespeare Birthplace Trust
Distributed in Canada by Sterling Publishing
c/o Canadian Manda Group, One Atlantic Avenue, Suite 105
Toronto, Ontario, Canada M6K 3E7
Distributed in Great Britain and Europe by Chris Lloyd
463 Ashley Road, Parkstone, Poole, Dorset, BH14 0AX, England
Distributed in Australia by Capricorn Link (Australia) Pty Ltd.
P.O. Box 6651, Baulkham Hills, Business Centre, NSW 2153, Australia
Printed in China

Sterling ISBN 0-8069-4344-0

CONTENTS

INTRODUCTION

William Shakespeare is the world's best-known dramatist. His plays have been performed more often—and more widely around the world—than those of any other playwright who ever lived. His writing has been translated into over 100 languages, and his plays and poems are sold in virtually every country.

"Shakespeare" is literally a household name. His first name, "William," is not needed to identify him. Shakespeare is the world's most famous writer, and there is never any doubt which Shakespeare is meant. Even a quickly drawn sketch—a broad-faced, middle-aged man with a high forehead and hair reaching just below his ears, especially if he is wearing a ruff around his neck and holding a quill pen—is usually instantly identifiable, even by those who have never read a word he has written.

His words are, however, what we know best about him. We quote him all the time, even when we are unaware of it. Many familiar words—"admirable," "attorney," "bedroom," "distasteful," "fashionable," "frugal," "laughable," "mimic," "solicit," "successful," "unreal," and "useful"—first appeared in print in his plays. Some of his phrases, like "at one fell swoop" or "sick at heart" are now so common they seem as if they have always been part of the language. Sentences that he wrote have become proverbial, seemingly timeless wisdom rather than the invention of some individual: "all the world's a stage"; "to thine own self be true"; "the course of true love never did run smooth."

We hear Shakespeare also from other mouths. His words have provided hundreds of writers with titles for books and films: William Faulkner's *The Sound and the Fury* (from *Macbeth*) and Aldous Huxley's *Brave New World* (from *The Tempest*), to name just two. His plots and characters have been the inspiration for many hundreds of artists. The Italian composer Verdi turned *Othello* into an opera, and Disney transformed *Hamlet* into *The Lion King*.

How has all this happened? How is it that his words still echo in our ears? How is it that not only has he become the inspiration for other artists but also that his art still inspires us? How is it that Shakespeare still speaks *to* us and often *for* us? How is it that we can hardly escape him, even now, well over four hundred years after his birth?

We read his plays in school, experience them in the theater, and now, increasingly, see them on video and the movie screen. In the last decade, ten full-length, feature films of his plays have been released, including *Romeo and Juliet*, starring Clare Danes and Leonardo DiCaprio. Shakespeare has a whole new generation of admirers.

There is no simple explanation for his popularity. He is our greatest entertainer and our most profound thinker. Though he wrote more than four centuries ago, Shakespeare, more than any other writer, is able to make us laugh and feel deeply. His plays and poems engage our hearts and our minds, exploring our most complex emotions and our most fundamental ideals, our fondest hopes and our most disturbing dreams.

Shakespeare didn't expect to have such a powerful effect or find such lasting fame. He had few literary ambitions, at least for his plays. He was a practical man of the theater: an actor, a playwright, and a part owner of the acting company for which he wrote. He was a member of a troupe of actors called the Lord Chamberlain's Men, which was renamed the King's Men soon after James succeeded Elizabeth on the throne of England in 1603.

During his career in the theater, Shakespeare became rich, but it was from the success of the acting company rather than from the sale of his plays. He received no direct payments for publication of any of them. He wrote them for actors to perform, not as texts to be published and read. Though nineteen of his plays were printed in his lifetime, not one was published with his involvement, nor even, perhaps, with his knowledge. Shakespeare seems not to have paid attention to these early printed playbooks. He cared only that the plays were successful on stage. The first seven actually appeared in print with no indication that Shakespeare was their author.

This is not, however, as surprising as it might seem. Plays then were very much like today's movies, a popular entertainment where star actors, rather than writers, attracted all the attention. Plays had not yet become a form of literature, and playwrights were not yet thought of as distinguished authors.

Only after his death was an effort made to publish a carefully edited volume of Shakespeare's collected plays. Two fellow actors, John Heminges and Henry Condell, joined with a group of publishers to produce a large and expensive edition, known today as the First Folio. This book, published in 1623, contains thirty-six of Shakespeare's plays, eighteen of which had not previously been published.

Heminges and Condell offered the book to the public with the aim, they said, not of achieving their own "self-profit" or "fame," but "only to keep the memory of so worthy a Friend and Fellow alive." And so they did.

After the publication of the First Folio, Shakespeare's artistic reputation and achievement were secure. Nonetheless, some people passionately believe that someone else was the author of Shakespeare's plays and poems. Little can be said for this view, except for the humor that it sometimes produces. Three prominent Anti-Stratfordians (those who deny Shakespeare's authorship) are men named Looney, Battey, and Silliman.

The argument that someone other than Shakespeare wrote the plays seems to be based on simple snobbery: a belief that only someone educated at court or at a university would be capable of such wonderful writing. But Shakespeare's life was not much different from that of the other major writers of his time. Like Shakespeare, most came from the lower middle class and most were not university educated.

We actually know a lot about Shakespeare, especially considering how long ago he lived. He was born in late April of 1564 in Stratford-upon-Avon, a small but prosperous market town in the middle of England, with wide streets and handsome houses roofed with thatch (straw). His father was John Shakespeare, a glovemaker and later a wool merchant, and his mother was Mary Arden, daughter of a successful farmer in the nearby village of Wilmcote. William was the third child of the eight they would eventually have. He was their firstborn son.

The parish church in Stratford records Shakespeare's baptism on April 26, so his birthday was probably three days earlier, on April 23. April 23 is St. George's Day, the holiday celebrating the patron saint of England, and it was also the date of Shakespeare's death in 1616, fifty-two years after he was born.

We believe that from about the age of five Shakespeare attended the local Stratford grammar school, whose rigorous curriculum was based largely on the study of Latin and the major classical writers. The school day was long; it began at six in the morning in the summer (seven in the winter) and lasted until early evening. School was usually open all year, except for major religious holidays. It closed for two weeks at Christmas, two weeks at Easter, and a week at Whitsuntide in early June.

We know for certain that at age 18 Shakespeare married Anne Hathaway, from the nearby village of Shottery. Their daughter, Susanna, was born on May 26, 1583. On February 2, 1585, Anne gave birth to twins: Hamnet, a boy, and Judith, a girl.

Sometime after the birth of the twins, Shakespeare left Stratford for London. There he began to prosper as both an actor and a playwright. There are many references to his activity in the theater. By 1598, a schoolmaster, Francis Meres, claimed that Shakespeare could be compared even with the great classical dramatists for tragedy and for comedy, and that among English writers he was "the best of both kinds for the stage." His plays were the most popular of his day, performed usually at the Globe Theater, which was built on the south bank of the River Thames in 1599.

His friends talked about his modesty and his good nature; scholars in his day commented on the excellence of his writing, and the contemporary court records revealed his prosperity. In 1597 he bought a substantial house in Stratford, known as New Place, for £60 (the equivalent today of about $50,000). In 1602, he purchased 107 acres north of the town for £320. In 1605 he bought a half-interest in a Stratford farm for £440, and in 1613, with three other investors, he acquired a house in Blackfriars, a district in London, for £140. These large sums of money reveal the considerable wealth he earned through his theatrical successes.

Shakespeare's work in the theater meant he spent most of the year in London. His family, however, remained in Stratford. Their lives and deaths can be traced through the Stratford parish register. His son, Hamnet, died at the age of eleven and was buried on August 11, 1596. Shakespeare's father died in September 1601, his mother in 1608. His elder daughter, Susanna, married John Hall, a well-respected Stratford physician, in Holy Trinity Church on June 5, 1607. His younger daughter, Judith, married Thomas Quiney on February 10, 1616. Shakespeare's wife died on August 6, 1623. She had lived to see a monument to her husband erected in Stratford's Holy Trinity Church, but died just before the publication of the first collected edition of his plays, the more important memorial to his greatness.

Shakespeare himself had died over seven years earlier, in late April of 1616. According to one report, his death came after a "merry meeting" with fellow writers, Ben Jonson and Michael Drayton, where Shakespeare "drank too hard." He was buried on the north side of the chancel of Holy Trinity Church.

His will has survived. He left £10 for "the poor of Stratford," remembered friends, and provided for his family. He left money for commorative rings to three surviving members of his acting company: Richard Burbage, John Heminges, and Henry Condell (the last two would later serve as the "editors" of the First Folio). He left £150 to his younger daughter, Judith, and another £150 to be paid if "she or any issue of her body be living" three years after the will was settled. But most of the estate was left to his older daughter, Susanna.

Oddly, Shakespeare's wife, Anne, is referred to only once in the will, in an apparent afterthought. Added between two lines of the document is: "Item, I give unto my wife my second best bed with the furniture" (the "furniture" was the bedding and canopy). Some people have seen this as a deliberate snub. Whether or not it was, Anne would not have been left penniless. English law usually provided the widow with one-third of the estate, which in Shakespeare's case was considerable. And leaving his wife their "second best bed" seems almost certainly a loving and sentimental gesture, assuring that the bed that was their own (the best being reserved for guests) remained her property.

What we know about Shakespeare's life can hardly explain his amazing accomplishment. No one has written poems and plays that have had such influence as Shakespeare's. No one has produced a body of writing that has been more admired or better loved. While today the poems, except for his *Sonnets*, are not often read, in Shakespeare's time the poetry was much admired. Francis Meres in 1598 referred to him as "mellifluous and honey-tongued Shakespeare," especially noting the popularity of "his *Venus and Adonis*, his *Lucrece*, his sugared Sonnets among his private friends."

But it is the plays that are Shakespeare's greatest artistic achievement. His dramatic career was long and uniquely successful. He wrote roughly two plays a year for eighteen straight years. Those plays prove he is, as his friend Ben Jonson said, "not of an age, but for all time."

In those wonderful plays—plays about love and jealousy, friendship and betrayal, politics and ambition, desire and death—he explores and celebrates the wondrous complexity of human life. His characters come alive for us. They make us believe in their reality and convince us to care about their fate. As Shakespeare shows us their struggles to understand their lives, he allows us to understand more about our own.

NOTE TO THE READER

Most of the selections in this book are lines spoken by a character in a play. But they are still poetry. Shakespeare's verse doesn't usually rhyme, but it has a definite rhythm. Most of the time his lines have ten syllables, and every other syllable is stressed—like this:

da-dum da-dum da-dum da-dum da-dum.

This is called *iambic pentameter*. Shakespeare often varies this basic pattern, though, for many different dramatic purposes.

FROM *A MIDSUMMER NIGHT'S DREAM*
ACT 5, SCENE 1, LINES 7–22

*Duke Theseus thinks about how imagination transforms
reality. For him, it distorts what the eye sees. But sometimes
the imagination may see truths that the eye cannot.*

The lunatic, the lover, and the poet
Are of imagination all compact:
One sees more devils than vast hell can hold;
That is the madman. The lover, all as frantic,
Sees Helen's beauty in a brow of Egypt.
The poet's eye, in a fine frenzy rolling,
Doth glance from heaven to earth, from earth
      to heaven;
And as imagination bodies forth
The forms of things unknown, the poet's pen
Turns them to shapes, and gives to airy nothing
A local habitation and a name.
Such tricks hath strong imagination,
That if it would but apprehend some joy
It comprehends some bringer of that joy;
Or, in the night, imagining some fear,
How easy is a bush supposed a bear!

compact—*composed*
Helen—*Helen of Troy*
brow of Egypt—*face of a gypsy*
bodies forth—*gives birth to*
habitation—*dwelling place*

Sonnet 18

A sonnet is a poem with fourteen lines and a set pattern of rhymes. Here the speaker compares his love to a summer day, and finds the human beauty "more lovely" and more lasting than nature's. But what finally insures that the youth's beauty will endure is that it is preserved for all time in the poem itself.

Shall I compare thee to a summer's day?
Thou art more lovely and more temperate.
Rough winds do shake the darling buds of May,
And summer's lease hath all too short a date.
Sometime too hot the eye of heaven shines,
And often is his gold complexion dimmed,
And every fair from fair sometime declines,
By chance or nature's changing course untrimmed.
But thy eternal summer shall not fade,
Nor lose possession of that fair thou ow'st;
Nor shall death brag thou wand'rest in his shade
When in eternal lines to time thou grow'st.
   So long as men can breathe or eyes can see,
   So long lives this, and this gives life to thee.

temperate—*mild*
lease—*allotted time*
eye of heaven—*the sun*
fair from fair—*beautiful person from that beauty*
untrimmed—*stripped of ornament*
ow'st—*own*

FROM *THE MERCHANT OF VENICE*
ACT 4, SCENE 1, LINES 182–195

Portia argues that mercy, even more than power, is the human quality that is most Godlike.

The quality of mercy is not strained.
It droppeth as the gentle rain from heaven
Upon the place beneath. It is twice blest:
It blesseth him that gives and him that takes.
'Tis mightiest in the mightiest; it becomes
The throned monarch better than his crown.
His scepter shows the force of temporal power,
The attribute to awe and majesty,
Wherein doth sit the dread and fear of kings.
But mercy is above this sceptred sway.
It is enthroned in the hearts of kings.
It is an attribute to God himself,
And earthly power doth then show likest God's
When mercy seasons justice.

strained—*forced, compelled*
becomes—*suits*
temporal—*governmental*
sceptred sway—*royal power*
attribute to—*quality of*
seasons—*moderates*

11

FROM *ANTONY AND CLEOPATRA*
ACT 2, SCENE 2, LINES 201–228

Enobarbus, a Roman friend of Antony's, describes the spectacular appearance of Cleopatra. This was the first time Marc Antony had ever set eyes on Cleopatra, and she was determined to dazzle him. She did; and Enobarbus here dazzles his Roman listeners with his account.

The barge she sat in, like a burnished throne,
Burned on the water. The poop was beaten gold,
Purple the sails, and so perfumed that
The winds were love-sick with them. The oars were silver,
Which to the tune of flutes kept stroke, and made
The water which they beat to follow faster,
As amorous of their strokes. For her own person,
It beggared all description: she did lie
In her pavilion, cloth-of-gold of tissue,
O'er picturing that Venus where we see
The fancy outwork nature. On each side her
Stood pretty dimpled boys, like smiling cupids,
With divers-colored fans, whose wind did seem
To glow the delicate cheeks which they did cool,
And what they undid did.

burnished—*glittering*
burned—*shone brightly*
poop—*upper deck*
cloth-of-gold of tissue—*cloth with gold threads woven in*
O'erpicturing—*more beautiful than*
fancy—*imagination*
divers-colored—*multicolored*
glow—*make glow*

12

FROM *THE TEMPEST*
ACT 1, SCENE 2, LINES 190–197

Prospero has ordered his spirit helper, Ariel, to raise up a great storm to terrify and bring to his island a group of Italian noblemen who have wronged him. Notice in Ariel's second speech how the rhythm of the lines corresponds to the quick movements that the spirit is describing.

ARIEL

All hail, great master! Grave sir, hail! I come
To answer thy best pleasure: be it to fly,
To swim, to dive into the fire, to ride
On the curled clouds. To thy strong bidding, task
Ariel and all his quality.

PROSPERO

Hast, thou, spirit,
Performed to point the tempest that I bade thee?

ARIEL

To every article.
I boarded the king's ship: now on the beak,
Now in the waist, the deck, in every cabin,
I flamed amazement; sometime I'd divide
And burn in many places: on the topmast,
The yards and bowsprit, would I flame distinctly,
Then meet and join. Jove's lightnings, the precursors
Of the dreadful thunder-claps, more momentary
And sight-outrunning were not. The fire and cracks
Of sulphurous roaring the most mighty Neptune
Seem to beseige and make his bold waves tremble,
Yea, his dread trident shake.

task—*make demands upon*
quality—*abilities*
to point—*in every detail*
beak—*bow of a ship*
waist—*midship*

flamed amazement—*struck terror by appearing as fire*
yards and bowsprit—*masts and poles holding the sails*
distinctly—*in different places*

sight-outrunning—*faster than the eye can see*
sulphurous—*(sulphur was used in explosive devices)*

14

FROM *HAMLET*

ACT 3, SCENE 1, LINES 56–88

Hamlet's speech is probably the most famous in all of literature. He thinks about how difficult life is but also about how the nature of death cannot be known. Caught between a present that is often painful and a future that is always unknown, Hamlet wonders how anyone can know what to do.

To be, or not to be, that is the question:
Whether 'tis nobler in the mind to suffer
The slings and arrows of outrageous fortune,
Or to take arms against a sea of troubles
And by opposing end them. To die, to sleep—
No more—and by a sleep to say we end
The heart-ache and the thousand natural shocks
That flesh is heir to. 'Tis a consummation
Devoutly to be wished. To die, to sleep;
To sleep, perchance to dream. Ay, there's the rub;
For in that sleep of death what dreams may come
When we have shuffled off this mortal coil
Must give us pause. There's the respect
That makes calamity of so long life.
For who would bear the whips and scorns of time,
The oppressor's wrong, the proud man's contumely,
The pangs of despised love, the law's delay,
The insolence of office, and the spurns
That patient merit of the unworthy takes,
When he himself might his quietus make
With a bare bodkin? Who would fardels bear,
To grunt and sweat under a weary life,
But that the dread of something after death,
The undiscovered country, from whose bourn
No traveller returns, puzzles the will,
And makes us rather bear those ills we have
Than fly to others that we know not of?
Thus conscience does make cowards of us all;
And thus the native hue of resolution
Is sicklied o'er with the pale cast of thought,
And enterprises of great pith and moment
With this regard their currents turn awry
And lose the name of action.

rub—*obstacle*

shuffled off—*cast aside*

mortal coil—*earthly life*

respect—*consideration*

contumely—*insolent abuse*

office—*bureaucracy*

spurns—*insults*

quietus—*end*

bodkin—*dagger*

fardels—*burdens*

bourn—*border*

native hue—*natural color*

sicklied o'er—*made sickly*

pith and moment—*profundity and importance*

SONNET 116

This is probably the best known of Shakespeare's sonnets. Here the speaker sets forth an ideal of true love as something permanent and never changing. The first line echoes the old form of the marriage service, in which the clergyman asked if any one in attendance knew of "any impediment" that would prevent the couple from being married.

Let me not to the marriage of true minds
Admit impediments. Love is not love
Which alters when it alteration finds,
Or bends with the remover to remove.
O no, it is an ever-fixed mark,
That looks on tempests and is never shaken.
It is the star to every wandering bark,
Whose worth's unknown, although his height be taken.
Love's not Time's fool, though rosy lips and cheeks
Within his bending sickle's compass come.
Love alters not with his brief hours and weeks,
But bears it out even to the edge of doom.
   If this be error and upon me proved,
   I never writ, nor no man ever loved.

impediments—*objections*
ever-fixed mark—*permanently established beacon*
wandering bark—*lost ship*
unknown—*beyond human measurement*
fool—*plaything*
compass—*range*
bears it out—*endures*
the edge of doom—*Judgment Day*

FROM *HENRY V*
ACT 4, SCENE 1, LINES 226–245

*Henry V thinks about the heavy burdens that come
with being king. He sees that he is not really different
from those he rules, except that "ceremony," the
magnificent display of his royal power, makes others
obey him.*

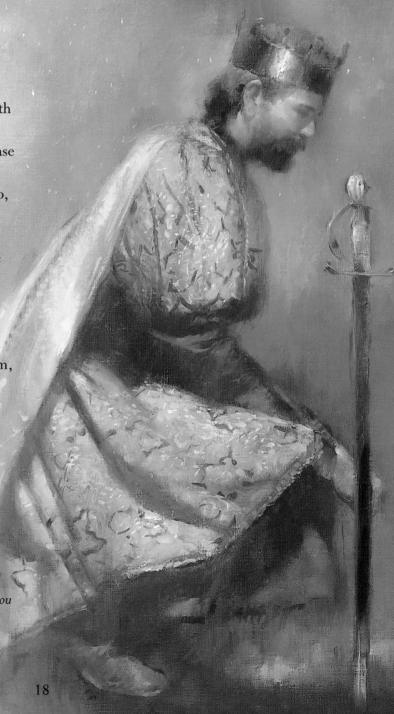

Upon the king! Let us our lives, our souls,
Our debts, our careful wives,
Our children, and our sins lay on the king!
We must bear all. O hard condition:
Twin-born with greatness, subject to the breath
Of every fool, whose sense no more can feel
But his own wringing! What infinite heart's-ease
Must kings neglect that private men enjoy!
And what have kings that privates have not too,
Save ceremony, save general ceremony?
And what art thou, thou idol ceremony?
What kind of god art thou, that suffer'st more
Of mortal griefs than do thy worshippers?
What are thy rents? What are thy comings-in?
O ceremony, show me but thy worth!
What is thy soul of adoration?
Are thou aught else but place, degree and form,
Creating awe and fear in other men,
Wherein thou art less happy being feared
Than they in fearing?

careful—*full of cares*
his own wringing—*what causes him pain*
privates—*ordinary citizens*
ceremony—*ceremonial display*
comings-in—*income*
thy soul of adoration—*essential quality that makes you
    admired*
place, degree and form—*position, status, and rank*

18

SONNET 29

*Feeling lonely and unsuccessful, the speaker of the poem
envies the talents and success of others. Then he suddenly
thinks about the person he loves and sees that this love more
than makes up for anything he lacks.*

When, in disgrace with fortune and men's eyes,
I all alone beweep my outcast state
And trouble deaf heaven with my bootless cries,
And look upon myself and curse my fate,
Wishing me like to one more rich in hope,
Featured like him, like him with friends possessed,
Desiring this man's art and that man's scope,
With what I most enjoy contented least;
Yet in these thoughts myself almost despising,
Haply I think on thee, and then my state,
Like to the lark at break of day arising,
From sullen earth sings hymns at heaven's gate.
    For thy sweet love remembered such wealth brings
    That then I scorn to change my state with kings.

state—*condition*
bootless—*useless*
Featured—*formed*
scope—*opportunities*
Haply—*by chance*
sullen—*dark*

FROM *MACBETH*

ACT 4, SCENE 1, LINES 1–21

The three witches, who earlier had prophesied that Macbeth would be king, now get ready for his visit. He comes to ask them what the future holds. They stir a pot filled with the unusual ingredients needed for their magic. The witches' verse is an eight-syllable, four-stress verse line, different from the human speakers (who all speak in Shakespeare's usual ten-syllable, five-stress line). Thus the witches' speech, as well as their appeareance, marks them as strange creatures.

FIRST WITCH
Thrice the brinded cat hath mewed.

SECOND WITCH
Thrice, and once the hedge-pig whined.

THIRD WITCH
Harpier cries. "'Tis time; 'tis time."

FIRST WITCH
Round about the cauldron go;
In the poisoned entrails throw.
Toad, that under cold stone
Days and nights has thirty-one
Sweltered venom sleeping got,
Boil thou first in the charmed pot.

ALL
Double, double, toil and trouble;
Fire burn, and cauldron bubble.

SECOND WITCH
Fillet of a fenny snake,
In the cauldron boil and bake;
Eye of newt and toe of frog,
Wool of bat and tongue of dog,
Adder's fork and blind worm's sting,
Lizard's leg, and howlet's wing,
For a charm of powerful trouble
Like a hell-broth boil and bubble.

ALL
Double, double, toil and trouble;
Fire burn, and cauldron bubble.

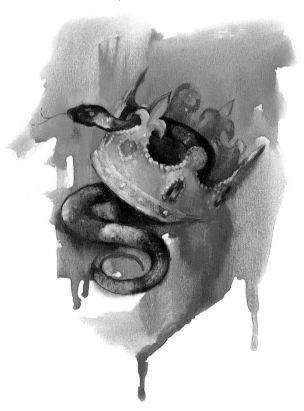

brinded—*streaked*
hedge-pig—*hedgehog*
Harpier—*the name of a spirit*
Days . . . got—*for thirty-one days and nights has exuded poison formed during sleep*
Fillet—*slice*
fenny—*from the swamp*
fork—*forked tongue*
howlet's—*owl's*

FROM *JULIUS CAESAR*
ACT 3, SCENE 2, LINES 74–108

This is Marc Antony's masterful funeral oration for Julius Caesar, which shows how a crowd can be manipulated by a skilled speaker. Notice the way in which Antony again and again calls Brutus "honorable," until it is quite clear that Antony thinks he is anything but.

Friends, Romans, countrymen, lend me your ears.
I come to bury Caesar, not to praise him.
The evil that men do lives after them;
The good is oft interred with their bones.
So let it be with Caesar. The noble Brutus
Hath told you Caesar was ambitious.
If it were so, it was a grievous fault,
And grievously hath Caesar answered it.
Here, under leave of Brutus and the rest—
For Brutus is an honorable man;
So are they all honorable men—
Come I to speak in Caesar's funeral.
He was my friend, faithful and just to me;
But Brutus says he was ambitious,
And Brutus is an honorable man.
He hath brought many captives home to Rome,
Whose ransoms did the general coffers fill.
Did this in Caesar seem ambitious?
When that the poor have cried, Caesar hath wept.
Ambition should be made of sterner stuff.
Yet Brutus says he was ambitious,
And Brutus is an honorable man.
You all did see that on the Lupercal
I thrice presented him a kingly crown,
Which he did thrice refuse. Was this ambition?
Yet Brutus says he was ambitious,
And sure he is an honorable man.
I speak not to disprove what Brutus spoke,
But here I am to speak what I do know.
You all did love him once, not without cause;
What cause withholds you then to mourn for him?
O judgment, thou art fled to brutish beasts,

And men have lost their reason. Bear with me.
My heart is in the coffin there with Caesar,
And I must pause till it come back to me.

answered—*paid the penalty for*
under leave—*by permission*
general coffers—*public treasury*
Lupercal—*a Roman holiday celebrated on February 15*

FROM *HENRY IV, PART ONE*
ACT 5, SCENE 1, LINES 131–141

Falstaff is an aging, fat knight, with an unquenchable zest for living. He has no interest in honor, which seems to him only a meaningless word. On the battlefield he tries only to avoid being killed. The speech is in prose. Falstaff never speaks verse in the play, resisting even that form of control.

FALSTAFF

Can honor set to a leg? No. Or an arm? No. Or take away the grief of a wound? No. Honor hath no skill in surgery then? No. What is honor? A word. What is in that word "honor"? What is that honor? Air. A trim reckoning. Who hath it? He that died a' Wednesday. Doth he feel it? No. Doth he hear it? No. 'Tis insensible, then? Yea, to the dead. But will it not live with the living? No. Why? Detraction will not suffer it. Therefore I'll none of it. Honor is a mere scutcheon. And so ends my catechism.

set to—*mend*
grief—*pain*
trim reckoning—*exact summing up*
Detraction—*malicious criticism*
mere scutcheon—*meaningless symbol*
catechism—*a series of questions
    and answers often used for religious
    instruction*

FROM *HENRY IV, PART ONE*

ACT 1, SCENE 2, LINES 190–212

The young Prince Hal has been spending all his time in the taverns of London drinking with Falstaff and other friends. Here, however, he reveals that this wild behavior has been carefully planned. He knows that one day he will become a worthy king; and, when he does, his bad reputation will make his royal conduct seem a miraculous transformation.

I know you all, and will awhile uphold
The unyoked humor of your idleness.
Yet herein will I imitate the sun,
Who doth permit the base contagious clouds
To smother up his beauty from the world,
That, when he please again to be himself,
Being wanted he may be more wondered at
By breaking through the foul and ugly mists
Of vapors that did seem to strangle him.
If all the year were playing holidays,
To sport would be as tedious as to work;
But when they seldom come, they wished for come,
And nothing pleaseth but rare accidents.
So when this loose behavior I throw off,
And pay the debt I never promised,
By how much better than my word I am,
By so much shall I falsify men's hopes.
And like bright metal on a sullen ground,
My reformation, glittering o'er my fault,
Shall show more goodly, and attract more eyes
Than that which hath no foil to set it off.
I'll so offend, to make offence a skill,
Redeeming time when men think least I will.

unyoked —*uncontrolled*
wanted—*missed*
rare accidents—*exceptional events*
hopes—*expectations*
sullen ground—*dark background*
foil—*contrasting background*
Redeeming time—*making amends for lost time*

FROM *AS YOU LIKE IT*
ACT 2, SCENE 7, LINES 174–193

Amiens, a lord who has accompanied the Duke into exile, sings this song. The Duke and his followers are living in the forest of Arden, having been banished from court by the Duke's evil brother. The song expresses sadness at this selfishness and ingratitude, but also a delight in their easy new life in the forest, even if it exposes them to the harshness of nature: "This life is most jolly!"

Blow, blow, thou winter wind,
Thou art not so unkind
   As man's ingratitude.
Thy tooth is not so keen,
Because thou art not seen,
   Although thy breath be rude.
Heigh-ho, sing heigh-ho, unto the green holly.
Most friendship is feigning, most loving mere
     folly.
Then heigh-ho, the holly!
   This life is most jolly.

Freeze, freeze, thou bitter sky,
That dost not bite so nigh
   As benefits forgot.
Though thou the waters warp,
Thy sting is not so sharp,
   As friend remembered not.
Heigh-ho, sing heigh-ho, unto the green holly,
Most friendship is feigning, most loving mere
     folly.
Then heigh-ho, the holly!
   This life is most jolly.

tooth—*bite*
rude—*rough*
feigning—*pretending*
nigh—*closely*
benefits forgot—*your generosity ignored*
warp—*freeze*

FROM *RICHARD II*
ACT 2, SCENE 1, LINES 40–50

*John of Gaunt, uncle of King Richard II, is dying. Here he
thinks of the glorious England he knew before Richard began
to exploit the country for his own selfish desires.*

This royal throne of kings, this sceptred isle,
This earth of majesty, this seat of Mars,
This other Eden, demi-paradise,
This fortress built by Nature for herself
Against infection and the hand of war,
This happy breed of men, this little world,
This precious stone set in the silver sea,
Which serves it in the office of a wall
Or as a moat defensive to a house
Against the envy of less happier lands;
This blessed plot, this earth, this realm, this England. . .

breed—*family*
office—*function*
envy—*malice*

FROM *THE TEMPEST*

ACT 1, SCENE 2, LINES 333–346

Prospero, the Duke of Milan, and his daughter, Miranda, were set adrift at sea, after Prospero was overthrown by his brother. Coming to a magical isle, they find Caliban, a creature half-man and half-fish, and at first treat him kindly. Now, however, Caliban complains about his treatment, claiming the island belongs by right to him.

This island's mine, by Sycorax my mother,
Which thou tak'st from me. When thou cam'st first,
Thou strok'st me and made much of me, wouldst give me
Water with berries in't, and teach me how
To name the bigger light, and how the less,
That burn by day and night. And then I loved thee,
And showed thee all the qualities of the isle:
The fresh springs, brine-pits, barren place and fertile:
Cursed be I that did so! All the charms
Of Sycorax—toads, beetles, bats—light on you!
For I am all the subjects that you have,
Which first was mine own King; and here you sty me
In this hard rock, whiles you do keep from me
The rest o' th' island.

strok'st—*stroked*
bigger light—*the sun*
the less—*the moon*
charms—*spells*
sty—*imprison*

FROM *A MIDSUMMER NIGHT'S DREAM*

ACT 5, SCENE 1, LINES 365–384

After much confusion throughout the play, three pairs of lovers, including Theseus and his Queen, Hippolyta, are about to be married. Here Puck, a mischievous spirit, prepares for the fairy blessing of these weddings, banishing all the threats to the lovers' happiness.

Now the hungry lion roars,
And the wolf behowls the moon;
Whilst the heavy ploughman snores,
All with weary task fordone.
Now the wasted brands do glow,
Whilst the screech-owl, screeching loud,
Puts the wretch that lies in woe
In remembrance of a shroud.
Now it is the time of night
That the graves, all gaping wide,
Every one lets forth his sprite
In the church-way paths to glide.
And we fairies, that do run
By the triple Hecate's team
From the presence of the sun,
Following darkness like a dream,
Now are frolic. Not a mouse
Shall disturb this hallowed house.
I am sent with broom before
To sweep the dust behind the door.

fordone—*worn out*
wasted brands—*burned-out logs*
shroud—*burial garment*
sprite—*ghost*

triple Hecate's team—*the team of dragons that brings the darkness, belonging to Hecate, the goddess of night; she is "triple" because she rules in heaven, earth, and hell.*
frolic—*merry*

FROM *RICHARD III*
ACT 5, SCENE 3, LINES 178–204

Richard wakes from a disturbing dream in which the ghosts of those he murdered appeared before him. Notice the jumpy and disjointed rhythms of the speech, as Richard tries to resist the knowledge of his villainy. But he must accept at last that he is a murderer and that no one loves or pities him—not even himself.

Give me another horse! Bind up my wounds!
Have mercy, Jesu! Soft! I did but dream.
O coward conscience, how dost thou afflict me!
The lights burn blue. It is now dead midnight.
Cold fearful drops stand on my trembling flesh.
What do I fear? Myself? There's none else by.
Richard loves Richard: that is, I am I.
Is there a murderer here? No. Yes. I am.
Then fly. What, from myself? Great reason why:
Lest I revenge. What, myself upon myself?
Alack, I love myself. Wherefore? For any good
That I myself have done unto myself?
O no! Alas, I rather hate myself
For hateful deeds committed by myself.
I am a villain. Yet I lie; I am not.
Fool, of thyself speak well. Fool, do not flatter.
My conscience hath a thousand several tongues,
And every tongue brings in a several tale,
And every tale condemns me for a villain.
Perjury, perjury, in the highest degree,
Murder, stern murder, in the direst degree,
All several sins, all used in each degree,
Throng to the bar, crying all, "Guilty! Guilty!"
I shall despair. There is no creature loves me;
And if I die, no soul will pity me.
And, wherefore should they, since that I myself
Find in myself no pity to myself?

Wherefore—*why*
several—*different*
Throng—*crowd together*
bar—*court*

30

FROM *HENRY V*

ACT 1, PROLOGUE, LINES 1–34

This is the prologue to Henry V, *setting the scene before the action of the play begins. The prologue apologizes for the fact that in the theater real kings and real armies are not available to act their parts. The spectators are told that their imaginations are as important as those of the playwright and the actors. The spectators must supply in their minds what can't be provided on stage.*

O for a muse of fire, that would ascend
The brightest heaven of invention!
A kingdom for a stage, princes to act
And monarchs to behold the swelling scene!
Then should the warlike Harry, like himself,
Assume the port of Mars; and at his heels,
Leashed in like hounds, should famine, sword, and fire
Crouch for employment. But pardon, gentles all,
The flat unraised spirits that have dared
On this unworthy scaffold to bring forth
So great an object. Can this cockpit hold
The vasty fields of France? Or may we cram
Within this wooden O the very casques
That did affright the air at Agincourt?
O, pardon! Since a crooked figure may
Attest in little place a million;
And let us, ciphers to this great account,
On your imaginary forces work.
Suppose within the girdle of these walls
Are now confined two mighty monarchies,
Whose high upreared and abutting fronts
The perilous narrow ocean parts asunder.
Piece out our imperfections with your thoughts;
Into a thousand parts divide one man,
And make imaginary puissance.
Think, when we talk of horses, that you see them
Printing their proud hoofs in the receiving earth.
For 'tis your thoughts that now must deck our kings,
Carry them here and there; jumping o'er times,
Turning the accomplishment of many years
Into an hourglass: for the which supply,

Admit me Chorus to this history,
Who, Prologue-like, your humble patience pray,
Gently to hear, kindly to judge, our play.

invention—*imagination*
swelling—*majestic*
Harry—*used here to refer familarly to King Henry V*
port—*manner*
gentles—*gentlemen and gentlewomen*
flat unraised spirits—*uninspired actors*
scaffold—*stage*
cockpit—*round arena for cockfighting (here, the round theater itself)*
vasty—*wide*
wooden O—*another reference to the round playhouse*
casques—*helmets*
Agincourt—*French locale where English troops led by Henry V won a remarkable victory over France*
crooked figure—*a zero (which added to the end of a number multiplies it by ten)*
attest—*stand for*
ciphers—*zeros*
imaginary forces—*powers of the imagination*
upreared—*raised up*
abutting—*touching*
fronts—*frontiers*
puissance—*armies*
deck—*equip*
supply—*service*

FROM *OTHELLO*
ACT 1.3.129–169

Othello explains how Desdemona came to love him. Her father has accused him of using witchcraft.

Her father loved me, oft invited me,
Still questioned me the story of my life
From year to year—the battles, sieges, fortunes
That I have passed.
I ran it through, even from my boyish days
To the very moment that he bade me tell it,
Wherein I spake of most disastrous chances,
Of moving accidents by flood and field,
Of hair breadth scapes i' th' imminent deadly breach,
Of being taken by the insolent foe
And sold to slavery; of my redemption thence
And portance in my travels' history,
Wherein of antres vast and deserts idle,
Rough quarries, rocks and hills whose heads touch heaven,
It was my hint to speak—such was my process—
And of the cannibals that each other eat,
The Anthropophagi, and men whose heads
Do grow beneath their shoulders. This to hear
Would Desdemona seriously incline;
But still the house affairs would draw her thence,
Which ever as she could with haste dispatch
She'd come again, and with a greedy ear
Devour up my discourse. Which I, observing,
Took once a pliant hour and found good means
To draw from her a prayer of earnest heart
That I would all my pilgrimage dilate,
Whereof by parcels she had something heard
But not intentively. I did consent,

Still—*constantly*
chances—*events*
scapes—*escapes*
imminent deadly breech—*dangerous gaps in the defenses*
insolent—*insulting*
portance—*behavior*
antres—*caves*

process—*story*
Anthropophagi—*man-eaters*
pliant—*convenient*
dilate—*relate*
intentively—*continuously*

And often did beguile her of her tears
When I did speak of some distressful stroke
That my youth suffered. My story being done
She gave me for my pains a world of sighs.
She swore in faith 'twas strange, 'twas passing strange,
'Twas pitiful, 'twas wondrous pitiful.
She wished she had not heard it, yet she wished
That heaven had made her such a man. She
      thanked me

And bade me, if I had a friend that loved her,
I should but teach him how to tell my story,
And that would woo her. Upon this hint I spake:
She loved me for the dangers I had passed
And I loved her that she did pity them.

passing—*exceptionally*
passed—*experienced*

FROM *MACBETH*
ACT 5, SCENE 5, LINES 19–28

Macbeth has become a murderer in order to make himself king. He finds, however, that his actions have not brought him the satisfaction he desired; in fact, they prevent him from gaining the respect and honor he seeks. And now all life has become just a meaningless sequence of days that can end only in death.

Tomorrow, and tomorrow, and tomorrow
Creeps in this petty pace from day to day,
To the last syllable of recorded time.
And all our yesterdays have lighted fools
The way to dusty death. Out, out, brief candle!
Life's but a walking shadow, a poor player,
That struts and frets his hour upon the stage,
And then is heard no more. It is a tale
Told by an idiot, full of sound and fury,
Signifying nothing.

FROM *TWELFTH NIGHT*
ACT 5, SCENE 1, LINES 381–400

The Clown, Feste, sings this song at the end of the play. It is a gloomy history of his growth from childhood. The repeated refrain, "the rain it raineth everyday," is a particularly bleak vision of the world, especially of a world that has provided the extraordinarily happy ending of the play. But Feste's account of the continuous rain is deliberately overstated, designed to make us aware of how much sunshine and delight there is in our lives.

When that I was and a little tiny boy,
   With hey, ho, the wind and the rain,
A foolish thing was but a toy,
   For the rain it raineth every day.

But when I came to man's estate,
   With hey, ho, the wind and the rain,
'Gainst knaves and thieves men shut their gate,
   For the rain it raineth every day.

But when I came, at last, to wive,
   With hey, ho, the wind and the rain,
By swaggering could I never thrive,
   For the rain it raineth every day.

But when I came unto my beds,
   With hey, ho, the wind and the rain,
With tosspots still had drunken heads,
   For the rain it raineth every day.

A great while ago the world begun,
   With hey, ho, the wind and the rain,
But that's all one, our play is done,
   And we'll strive to please you every day.

swaggering—*bullying*
beds—*sickbed*
tosspots—*drunkards*

FROM *HAMLET*
ACT 4, SCENE 7, LINES 166–183

*Queen Gertrude movingly tells of Ophelia's tragic death.
Ophelia, driven mad by her father's death and Hamlet's
rejection of her, wandered down to a brook, singing bits of
old songs and crowned with a garland of flowers she had
made. Falling into the water, she drowned as her water-
logged dress dragged her down. Gertrude's description has
inspired a number of famous paintings of Ophelia's death,
the best known being by Dante Gabriel Rossetti.*

There is a willow grows askant the brook,
That shows his hoar leaves in the glassy stream.
Therewith fantastic garlands did she make
Of crow-flowers, nettles, daisies, and long purples,
That liberal shepherds give a grosser name,
But our cold maids do dead men's fingers call them.
There on the pendant boughs her crownet weeds
Clambering to hang, an envious sliver broke,
When down her weedy trophies and herself
Fell in the weeping brook. Her clothes spread wide,
And mermaid-like awhile they bore her up,
Which time she chanted snatches of old lauds,
As one incapable of her own distress,
Or like a creature native and indued
Unto that element. But long it could not be
Till that her garments, heavy with their drink,
Pulled the poor wretch from her melodious lay
To muddy death.

askant—*leaning over* envious sliver—*malicious*
hoar—*white*   *branch*
long purples—*a kind of* lauds—*hymns*
 wild orchid   incapable—*uncomprehending*
liberal—*free-spoken* indued—*naturally adapted*
pendant—*overhanging* lay—*song*
crownet weeds—*weeds*
 made into a garland

FROM KING LEAR

ACT 3, SCENE 2, LINES 1–9

King Lear has divided his kingdom between two of his daughters, Goneril and Regan, and they have both abandoned him. Wandering on a barren heath in the midst of a fierce storm, he calls on all the forces of nature to destroy everything in his great rage at his mistreatment by his ungrateful daughters.

Blow winds and crack your cheeks! Rage, blow!
You cataracts and hurricanoes spout
Till you have drenched our steeples, drowned the cocks!
You sulphurous and thought-executing fires,
Vaunt-couriers of oak-cleaving thunderbolts,
Singe my white head! And thou, all-shaking thunder,
Strike flat the thick rotundity o' the world,
Crack nature's molds, all germens spill at once
That make ingrateful man!

cataracts and hurricanoes—*floods and water-*
    spouts
cocks—*weathervanes*
thought-executing fires—*the lightning that he*
    wants to carry out his threats
Vaunt-couriers—*forerunners*
rotundity—*roundness*
germens—*seeds*

FROM *THE TEMPEST*
ACT 5, SCENE 1, LINES 33–57

Prospero, a powerful magician, addresses the spirits that serve him and thinks about his extraordinary powers. But having accomplished what he has set out to do—bring those who had wronged him into his power and force their repentance—he promises to abandon all sorcery.

Ye elves of hills, brooks, standing lakes, and groves,
And ye that on the sands with printless foot
Do chase the ebbing Neptune, and do fly him
When he comes back; you demi-puppets that
By moonshine do the green sour ringlets make,
Whereof the ewe not bites; and you whose pastime
Is to make midnight mushrooms, that rejoice
To hear the solemn curfew; by whose aid,
Weak masters though ye be, I have bedimmed
The noontide sun, called forth the mutinous winds,
And 'twixt the green sea and the azured vault
Set roaring war. To the dread rattling thunder
Have I given fire, and rifted Jove's stout oak
With his own bolt. The strong based promontory
Have I made shake, and by the spurs plucked up
The pine and cedars. Graves at my command
Have waked their sleepers, op'd, and let 'em forth
By my so potent art. But this rough magic
I here abjure, and, when I have required
Some heavenly music, which even now I do,
To work mine end upon their senses that
This airy charm is for, I'll break my staff,
Bury it certain fathoms in the earth,
And deeper than did ever plummet sound
I'll drown my book.

demi-puppets—*tiny spirits*
green sour ringlets—*circles that appear in the grass, often called fairy circles*
bedimmed—*darkened*
azured vault—*sky*
rifted—*split*
promontory—*mountain top*
bolt—*lightning bolt*
spurs—*roots*
op'd—*opened*
abjure—*reject*
required—*summoned*
fathoms—*units of length each equal to six feet*
plummet—*a weighted line for measuring depth*

FROM *HENRY V*

ACT 4, SCENE 3, LINES 40–67

Henry V's stirring speech seeks to comfort and inspire his small band of gallant soldiers before the battle at Agincourt. His troops are heavily outmanned by the powerful French army. He promises them, however, that the story of their bravery shall be celebrated forever in England.

This day is called the feast of Crispian.
He that outlives this day and comes safe home
Will stand a tiptoe when this day is named
And rouse him at the name of Crispian.
He that shall see this day and live t'old age
Will yearly on the vigil feast his neighbors,
And say, "Tomorrow is Saint Crispian."
Then he will strip his sleeve and show his scars,
And say "These wounds I had on Crispin's day."
Old men forget; yet all shall be forgot,
But he'll remember, with advantages
What feats he did that day. Then shall our names,
Familiar in his mouth as household words—
Harry the King, Bedford and Exeter,
Warwick and Talbot, Salisbury and Gloucester—
Be in their flowing cups freshly remembered.
This story shall the good man teach his son,
And Crispin Crispian shall ne'er go by
From this day to the ending of the world
But we in it shall be remembered:
We few, we happy few, we band of brothers.
For he today that sheds his blood with me
Shall be my brother. Be he ne'er so vile,
This day shall gentle his condition.
And gentlemen in England now abed
Shall think themselves accursed they were not here,
And hold their manhoods cheap whiles any speaks
That fought with us upon Saint Crispin's day.

feast of Crispian—*St. Crispin's Day, October 25*
vigil—*the night before a holiday*
advantages—*embellishments*
vile—*low-born*
gentle his condition—*raise him to the rank of gentleman*

FROM *ROMEO AND JULIET*
ACT 1, SCENE 4, LINES 53–71

Mercutio mocks the lovesick Romeo with his story of the miniature Queen Mab. Probably Shakespeare's own invention,
Queen Mab is the fairy responsible for the strange behavior of those in love.

O, then, I see Queen Mab hath been with you.
She is the fairies' midwife, and she comes
In shape no bigger than an agate stone
On the forefinger of an alderman,
Drawn with a team of little atomies
Over men's noses as they lie asleep.
Her chariot is an empty hazelnut
Made by the joiner squirrel or old grub,
Time out o' mind the fairies' coachmakers.
Her wagon-spokes made of long spinners' legs,
The cover of the wings of grasshoppers,
Her traces of the smallest spider web,
Her collars of the moonshine's watery beams,
Her whip of cricket's bone, the lash of film,
Her wagoner a small grey-coated gnat,
Not half so big as a round little worm
Pricked from the lazy finger of a maid.
And in this state she gallops night by night
Through lovers' brains, and then they dream of love.

midwife—*one who assists in childbirth*
alderman—*a member of a city council*
atomies—*tiny creatures*
joiner—*carpenter*
Time out o' mind—*as long as anyone can remember*
spinners—*spiders*
traces—*harnesses*
film—*spider-web thread*
wagoner—*wagon driver*

FROM *AS YOU LIKE IT*
ACT 2, SCENE 7, LINES 139–166

The melancholy Jaques sees the seven stages of human life as an irresistible movement towards decay. The speech is justly famous but should not be taken as Shakespeare's own vision of life. The play itself offers too many examples of human kindness and love for Jaques's memorable pessimism to do more than amuse us.

All the world's a stage,
And all the men and women merely players.
They have their exits and their entrances,
And one man in his time plays many parts,
His acts being seven ages. At first the infant,
Mewling and puking in the nurse's arms.
Then, the whining school-boy with his satchel
And shining morning-face, creeping like snail
Unwillingly to school. And then the lover,
Sighing like furnace, with a woeful ballad
Made to his mistress's eyebrow. Then a soldier,
Full of strange oaths and bearded like the pard,
Jealous in honor, sudden, and quick in quarrel,
Seeking the bubble reputation
Even in the cannon's mouth. And then the justice,
In fair round belly, with good capon lined,
With eyes severe and beard of formal cut,
Full of wise saws, and modern instances.
And so he plays his part. The sixth age shifts
Into the lean and slippered pantaloon,
With spectacles on nose and pouch on side,
His youthful hose well saved, a world too wide
For his shrunk shank; and his big manly voice,
Turning again toward childish treble, pipes
And whistles in his sound. Last scene of all,
That ends this strange eventful history,
Is second childishness and mere oblivion,
Sans teeth, sans eyes, sans taste, sans everything.

		instances—*examples*
mewling—*crying*	capon—*fattened chicken*	pantaloon—*feeble old man*
pard—*leopard*	lined—*stuffed*	shank—*calf*
jealous—*is jealous about*	saws—*sayings*	sans—*without*

INDEX